PIANO SOLO

A CHARLIE BROWN CHRISTMAS™

ISBN 978-0-634-02979-0

HAL•LEONARD®
CORPORATION
7777 W. BLUEMOUND RD. P.O. BOX 13819 MILWAUKEE, WI 53213

PEANUTS © United Feature Syndicate, Inc.
www.snoopy.com

Visit Hal Leonard Online at
www.halleonard.com

CONTENTS

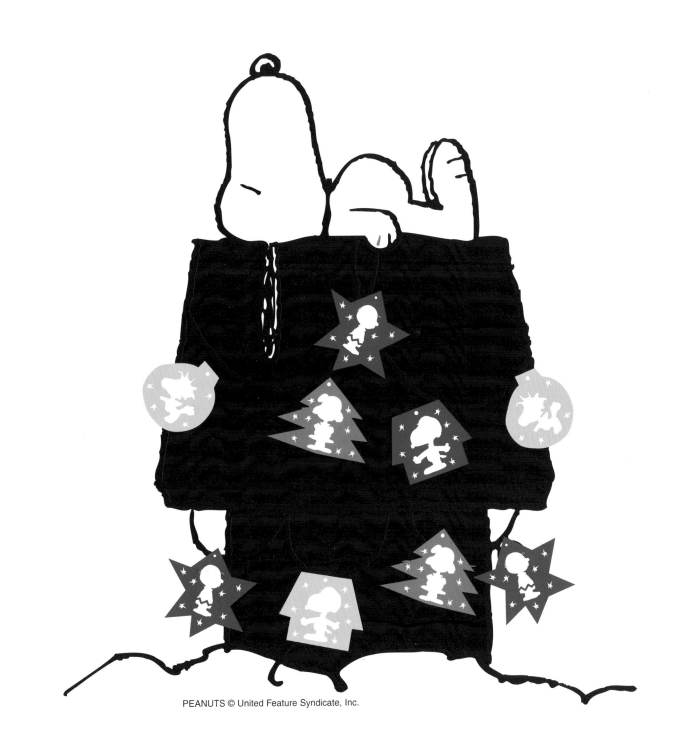

PEANUTS © United Feature Syndicate, Inc.

O TANNENBAUM

Traditional
Arranged by VINCE GUARALDI

Freely

With pedal

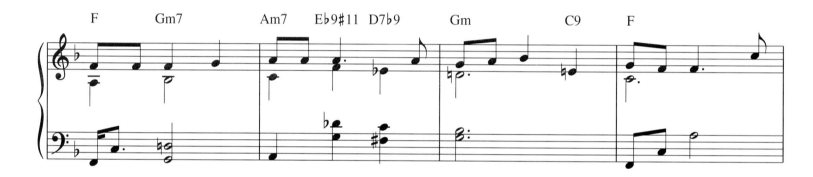

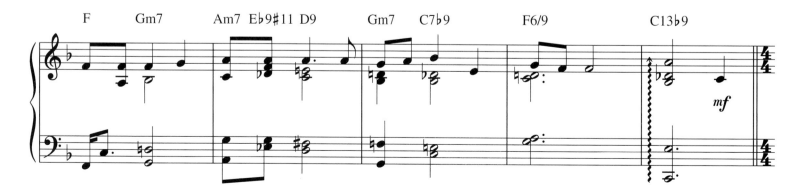

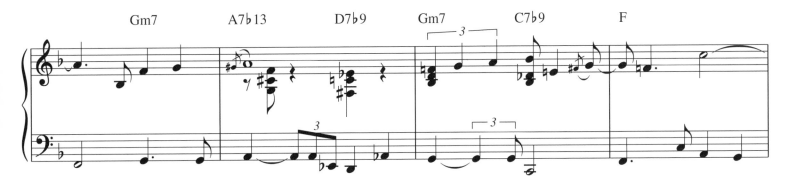

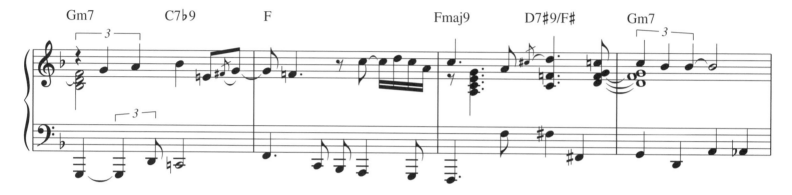

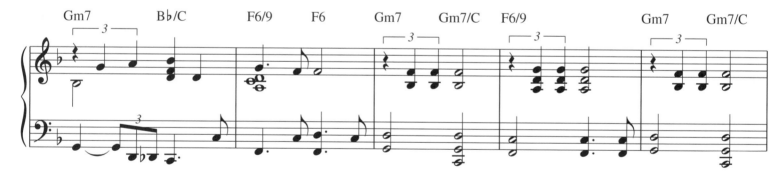

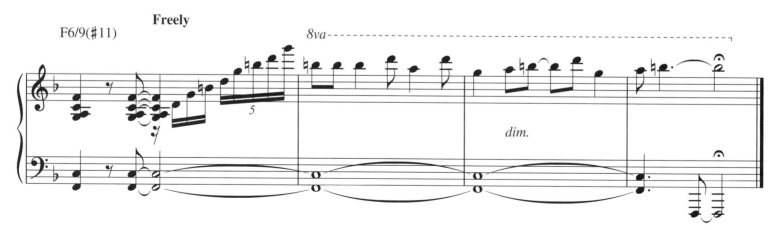

WHAT CHILD IS THIS

Traditional
Arranged by VINCE GUARALDI

Moderately slow Jazz Waltz

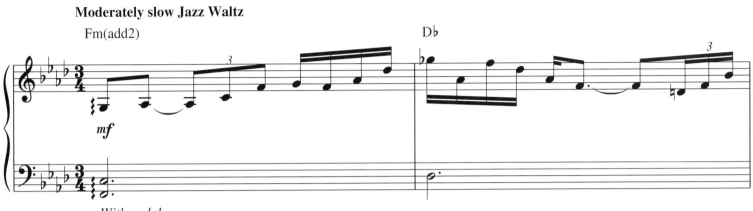

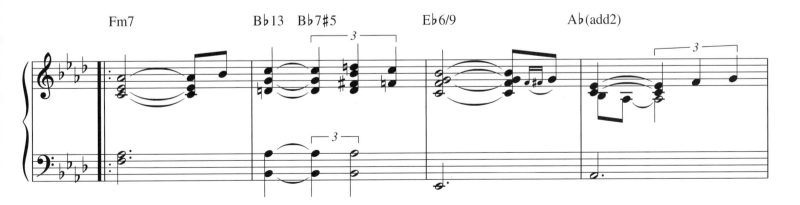

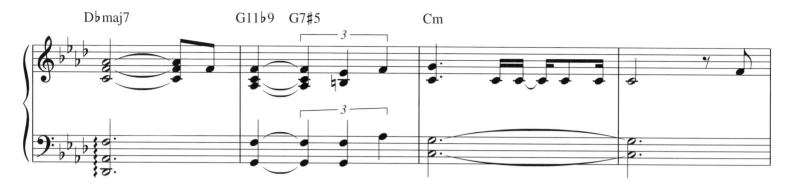

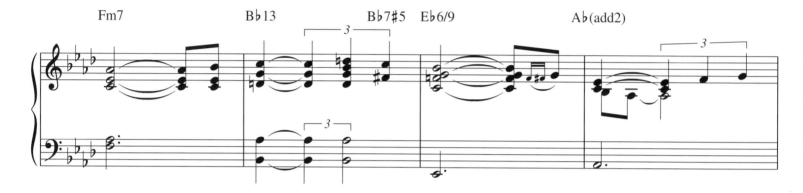

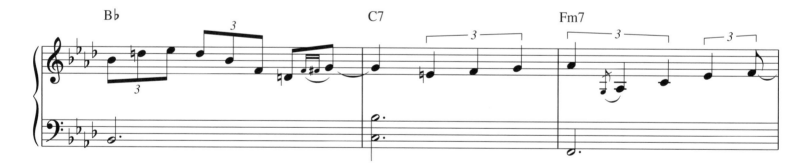

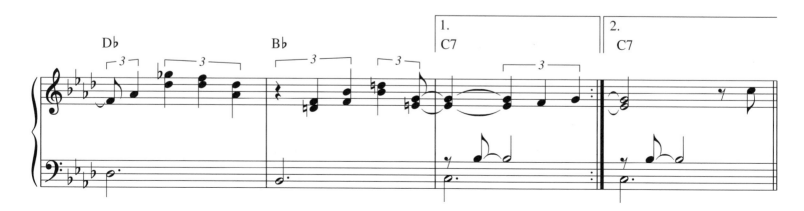

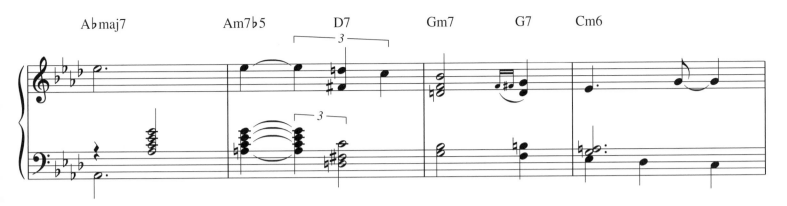

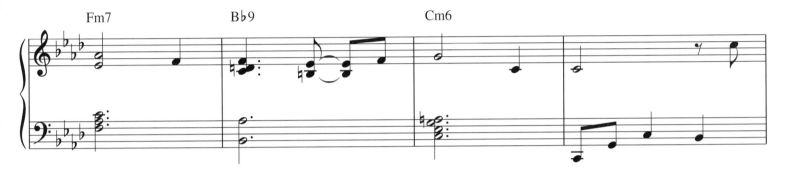

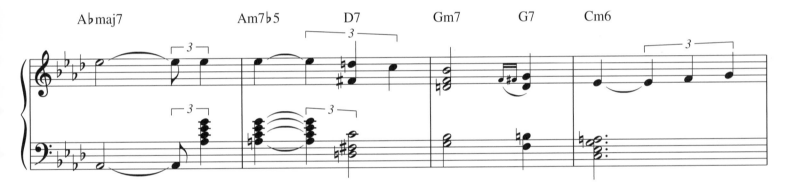

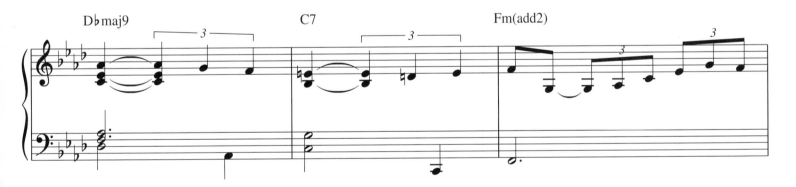

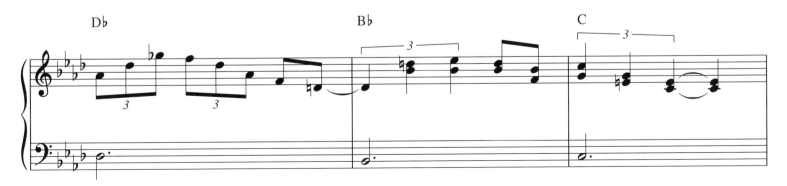

14

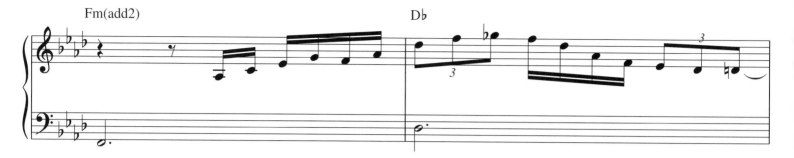

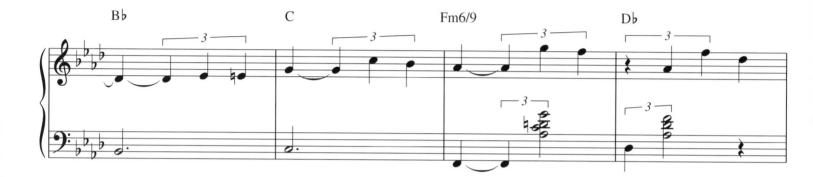

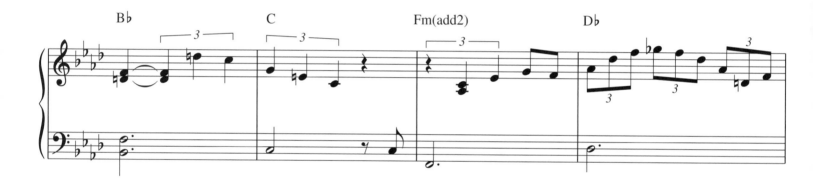

MY LITTLE DRUM

By VINCE GUARALDI

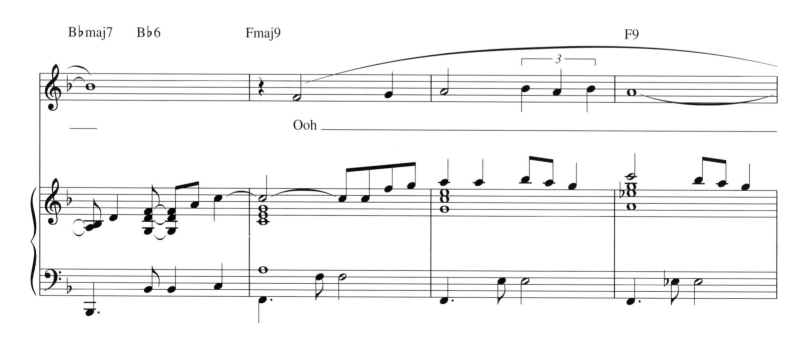

Bm7♭5   B♭m6   F/A   A♭m7   Gm7   B♭m/C   Fmaj9

D.S. al Coda

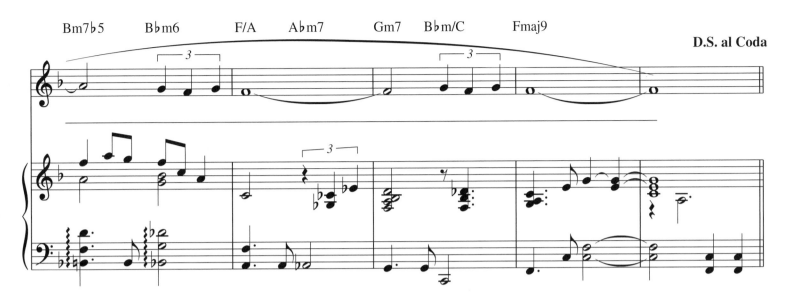

CODA

N.C./F

Repeat and Fade | **Optional Ending**

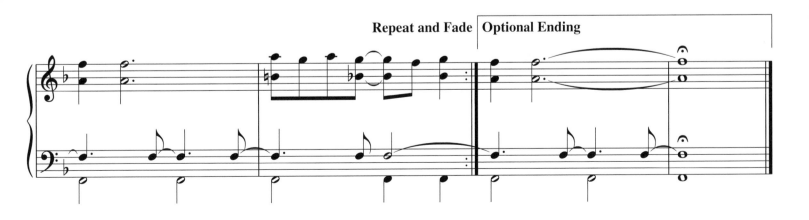

LINUS AND LUCY

By VINCE GUARALDI

Moderately fast

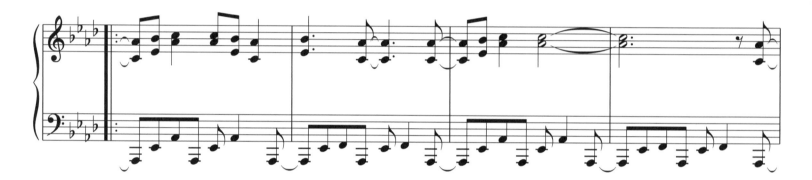

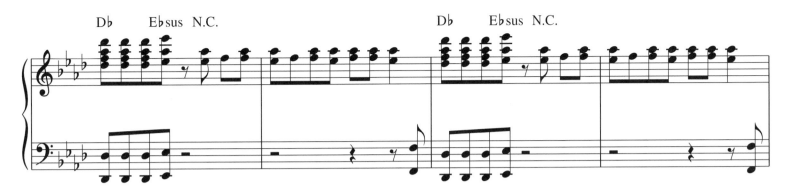

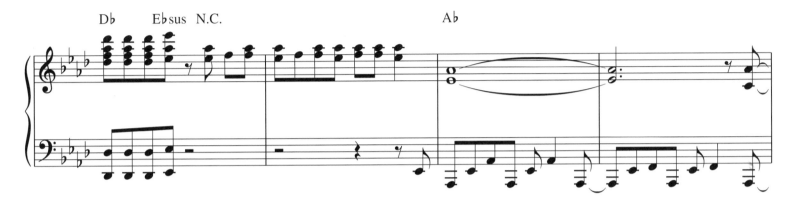

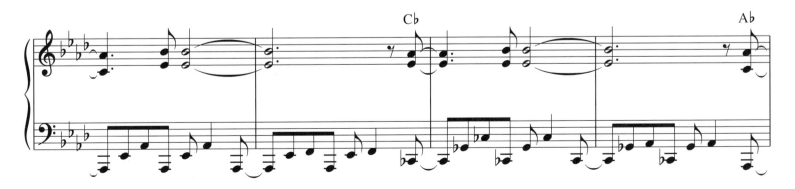

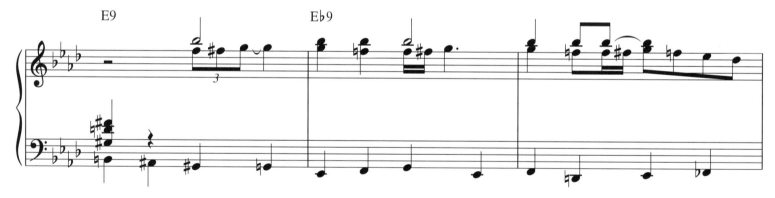

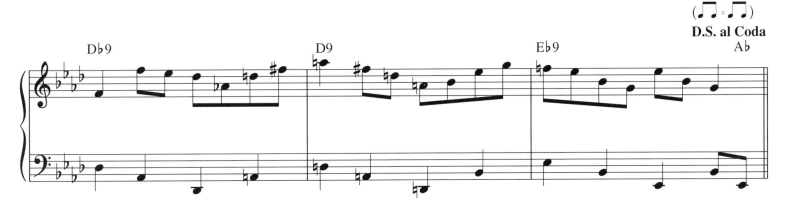

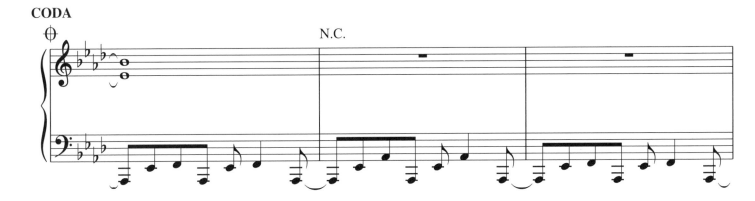

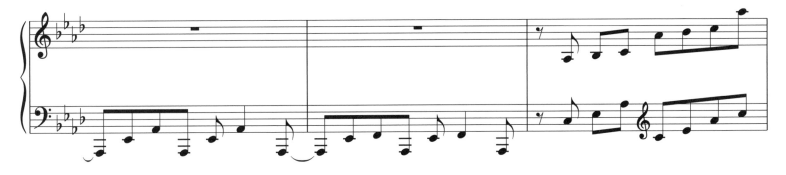

CHRISTMAS TIME IS HERE

Words by LEE MENDELSON
Music by VINCE GUARALDI

Christ - mas time is here, hap - pi - ness and
Snow - flakes in the air, car - ols ev - 'ry -

cheer. Fun for all that chil - dren call their
where. Old - en times and an - cient rhymes their

fa - v'rite time of year.
love and dreams to share.

26

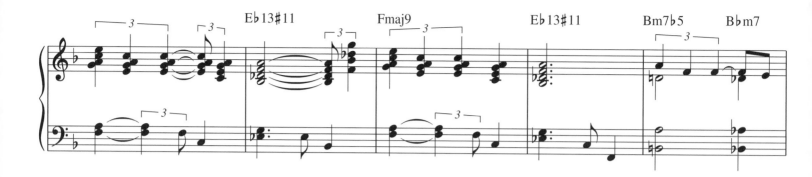

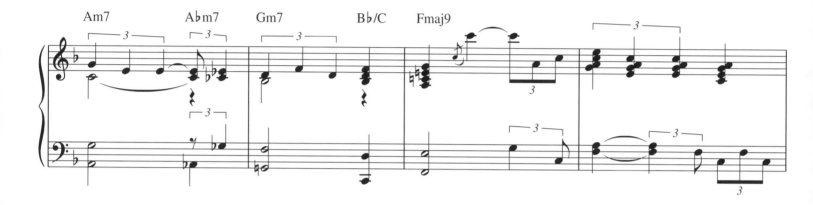

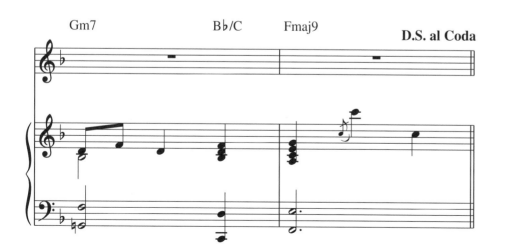

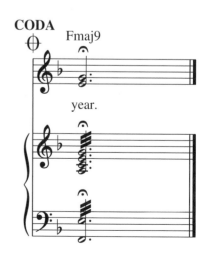

SKATING

By VINCE GUARALDI

Bright Jazz Waltz

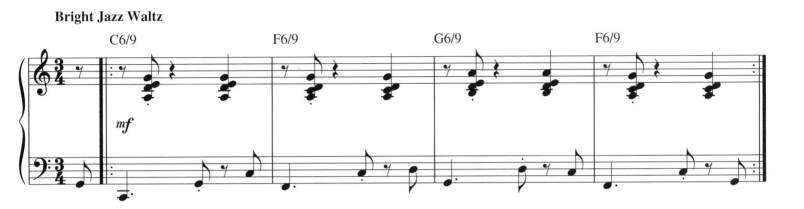

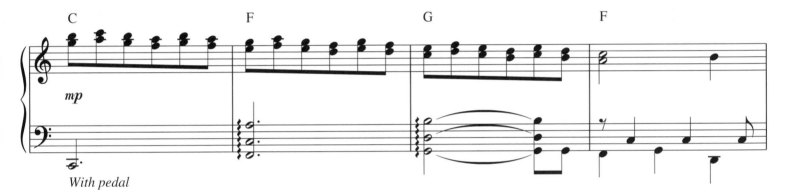

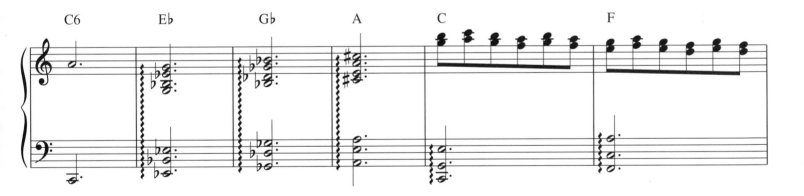

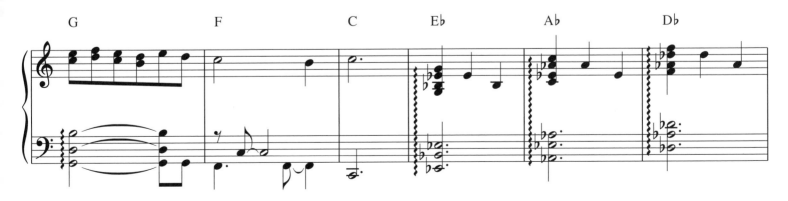

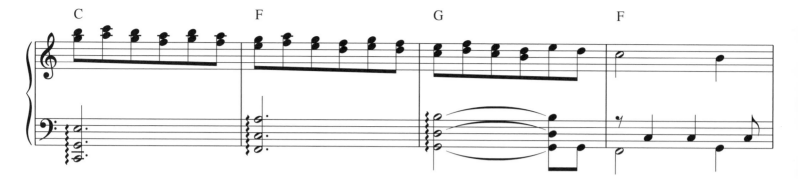

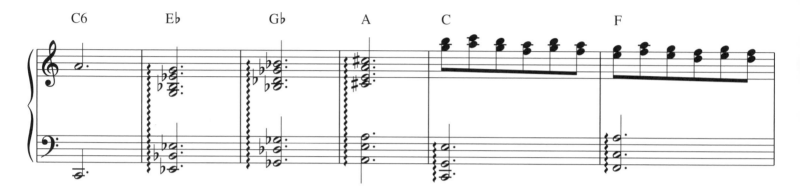

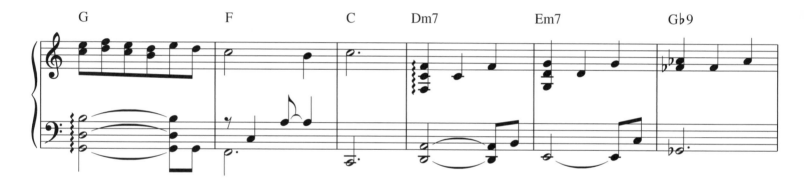

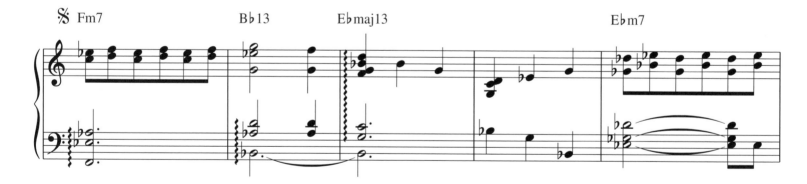

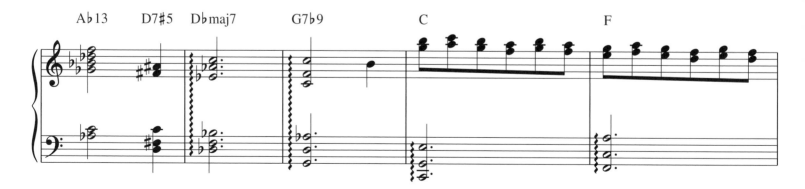

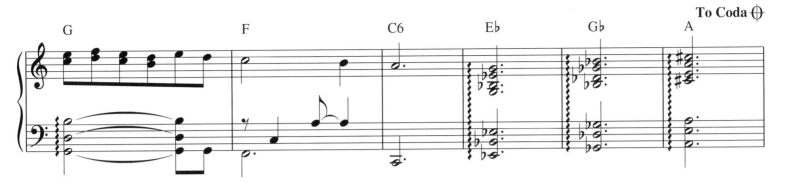

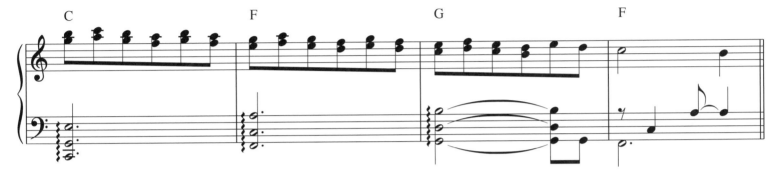

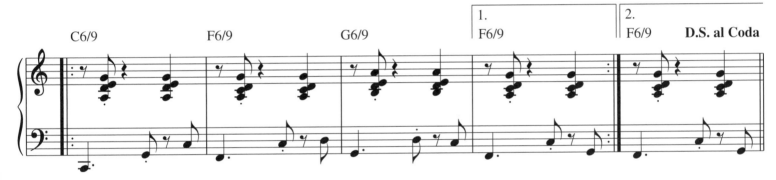

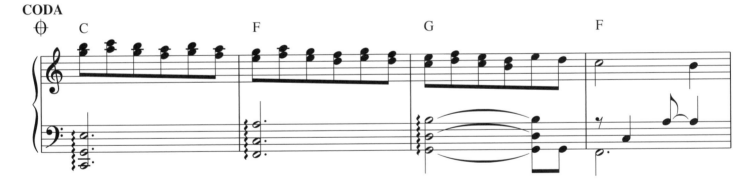

HARK, THE HERALD ANGELS SING

Traditional
Arranged by VINCE GUARALDI

CHRISTMAS IS COMING

By VINCE GUARALDI

Bright Bossa, Rock feel

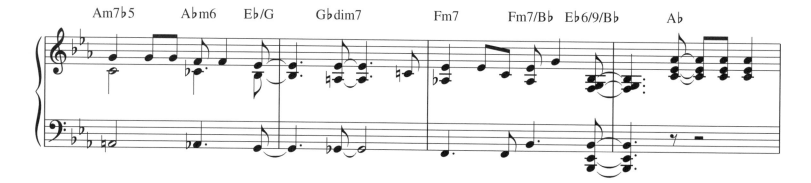

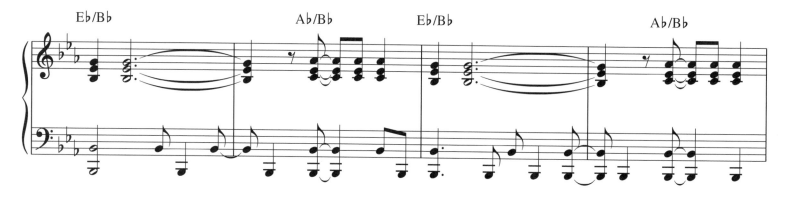

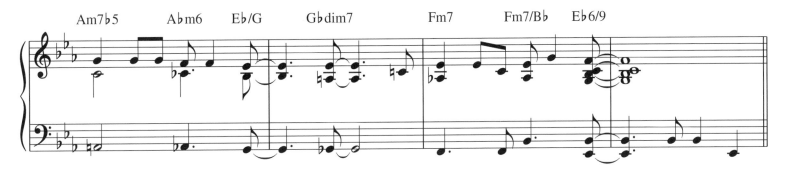

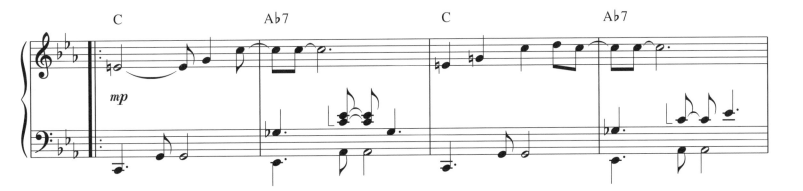

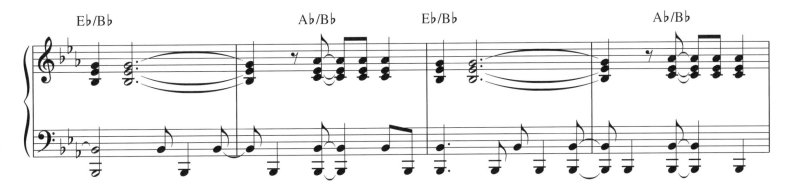

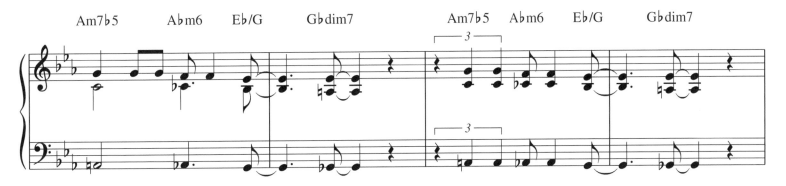

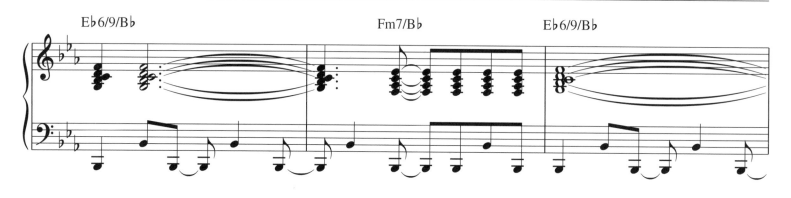

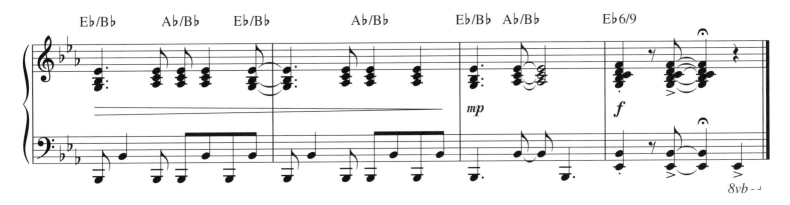

FÜR ELISE

By BEETHOVEN
Arranged by VINCE GUARALDI

Poco moto

THE CHRISTMAS SONG
(Chestnuts Roasting on an Open Fire)

Music and Lyric by MEL TORME
and ROBERT WELLS

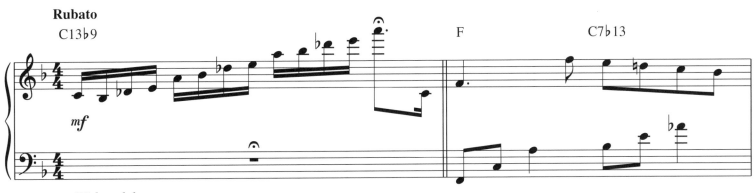

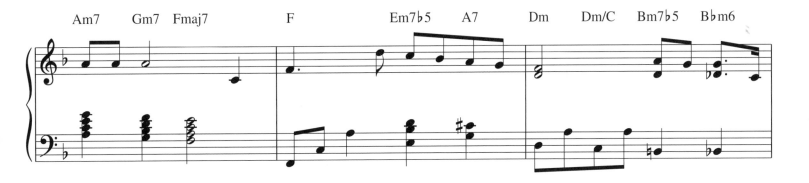

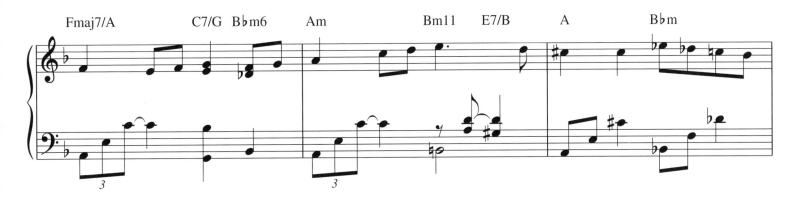

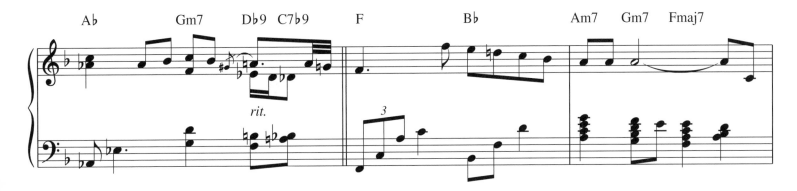

38

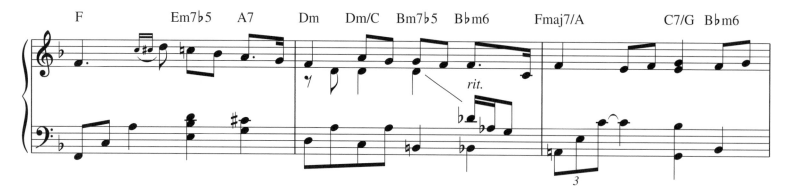

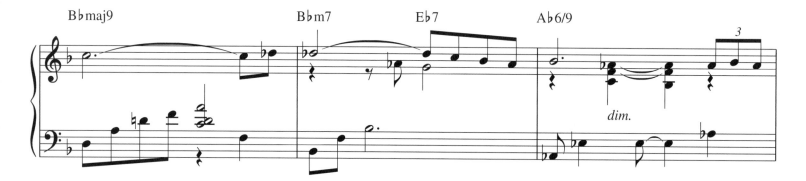

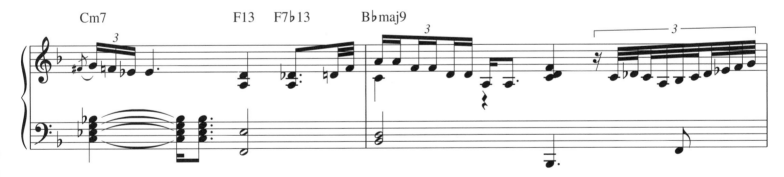

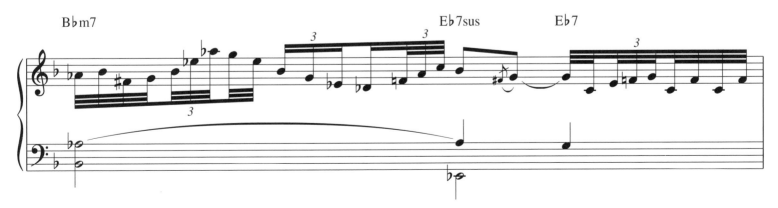

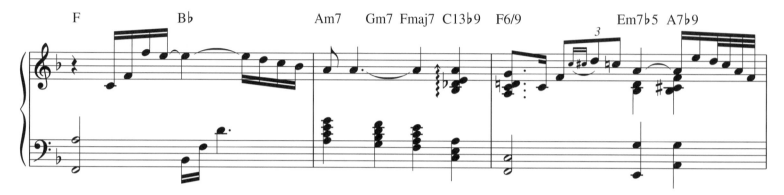

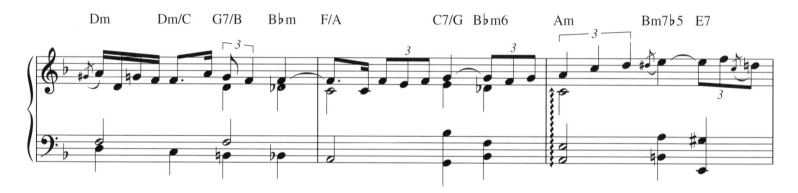

Rubato

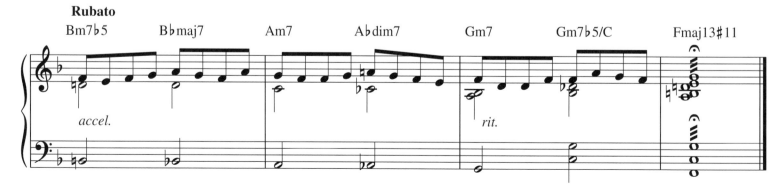